lavender field in me

[the internally passioned [trusting[tender[truthful[true blue humble [compassionate [curious [courageous [zestful inner beauty deep within the child at play in the field of lavender hue[is of great worth to the one true god[the me of the trust[tenderness[truth

[lamal[lavender[lovnew[
[me[the one true god[the me[humanity[

published by: the we of all humanity
6101Morris Street, Apt 216
Philadelphia, PA 19144

International Standard Book Number, ISBN: 978-0-9915187-6-0
ISBN-10: 0991518764

to be printed in-"The-"(United-States-Of-America)"

page guide

introduction

"Th(e)" - (Non-"(Con)"-ventional)"-Writing)"-Style), " (Use)"-Of" - (Co-"(L)"-oR)" - "(Cod(e)-ing)" - is used in numerous adult books written by the author on various topics, including ; the scientific proof of the one true god the me postulate , the simple integrated truth, society by design , "(Columbine)" - why - "(Children)"-Are-"(Killing)" - "(Children)", 'H-A-D,' "The- (My)"-Myth)," '{(S-LAUGHTER}}.' the books are written in a modified version because combining all of the elements makes the text virtually unreadable . the simple truth is regardless of the topic being discussed in any of the books , "Th(e)" - (Non-"(Con)"-ventional)"-Writing)"-Style), " (Use)"-Of" - "(Co-"(L)"-oR)" - (Cod(e)-ing)" helps create understanding by visually supporting the intended message.

both - "Th(e)" - (St-Y-L(e)" - using all of the elements, the modified version of - "The- "(Style)" - are intended to help the reader better understand ; "The- "(Generational)" effect)"-Of) - (Bl-A-cK Wh-I-T(e)" - "(Parenting)" - (With-"(Fear)," "(A) - "(Lack)"- Of)" - lamal - "(before-the-age-of-two)," the simple truth integrated into the language of humanity by the creator of humanity , as well as the vibrationally sensitive universe within the one true god the me of the trust tenderness truth . while - "The-"(Co-"(L)"- oR)" - (Cod(e)-ing)"-Table) - on page 25 explains the meaning for each of the colors used in - "The- "(Style)," a brief description for each of the text elements associated with - "Th(e)" - (Non-"(Con)"-ventional)"-Writing)"-Style), " (Use)"-Of" - (Co-"(L)"- oR)" - (Cod(e)-ing) - listed below are described in more detail in the following pages .

the integral symbol, "(Capitalization)," "The-"(Parentheses)," 'THE- '[BRACKETS],' 'THE-'{BRACES},' the dash, "(Double)" -'[(SINGLE)}'- set of quotation marks, the - "(Forward-VERTICAL-BACKWARD)}'- slashes, "The-"(elimination)"-Of-"(Many)"-Pronouns)," "The-"(Restricted)"- Use)"-Of-"(Possessive)"-Words)," "The-"(elimination)"-Of-"(Con)"-tractions)," the elimination of - "The-"(Major-"(Con)"-junctions)," "(And) - "(But)" - "(Or)," not following the grammatical rule of eliminating - "The-"(e)"- if adding a suffix, the simple truth is because sentence structure, "(Substituting-"(Con)"-For)"- com, "(Word)"-Separation)," "The-"(Inter-"(R(e)-lationship)"- between words.

using a modified version of - "The-"(Style)"- to help the reader understand - "The- "(Generational)"-effect)"-Of) - (Bl-A-cK Wh-I-T(e)" - "(Parenting)" - (With-"(Fear)," "(A) - "(Lack)"-Of)" - lamal - "(before-the-age-of-two)" - is critical because - "The- "(Generational)"-effect)"-Of) - (Bl-A-cK Wh-I-T(e)" - "(Parenting)" - (With-"(Fear),"

"(A)" - "(Lack)"-Of)" - ∫amal∫ - "(before-the-age-of-two)" - ∫is the cause of∫ - "The- "(emotional∫Physical)"-Pain/Suffering)" - ∫on∫the home planet∫. ∫the use of∫ - "The- "(Style)" - ∫in∫ - "(Columbine)" - ∫why∫ - "(Children"-Are-"(Killing)" - "(Children)" - ∫for example answers the question of nature∫versus∫nurture∫because∫ - "The- "(emotional∫Intellectual)"-Divide)"-Within)"-"(Allowing)" - "(Children"-To-"(Kill)" - "(Children)," as occurred at∫ - "The- "(Columbine- "(Killing)"-Field)" - ∫is not caused by the inability of the creator to integrate the qualities of being trusting∫tender∫truthful into ∫the gene code of humanity∫.

the simple integrated truth is∫combining all of the elements in∫ - "Th(e)" - "(Non-"(Con)"- ventional)"-Writing)"-Style)," "(Use)"-Of)" - "(Co-"(L)"-oR)" - "(Cod(e)-ing)" - ∫gives the reader a sense of the difference between being emotionally∫intellectually balanced∫, "(B(e)-"(I)"-nG)" - "(S(e)-V(e)-R(e)-lY)"-"(eI)"-"(Un-"(BaL-"(A)"-Nc(e)"-(e)D)" - ∫because unlike∫ - "The-"(nO)"-WiL)"-BiL)"-Ability)" - ∫of∫ - "(Untrue)"-Blue)" - Humanity)" - ∫to∫ - "(Use)" - "The- "(Boy"-"God"-"Con"-"Ta/Al)"-"(Denial)"-Matrix)"-To- "(Deny)"-Being)" - "(S(e)-V(e)-R(e)-lY)"-"(e)M-Ot-I-On-Al-lY∫In-T(e)-ll-(e)C-tU-Al- lY)"-"(Un-"(BaL-"(A)"-Nc(e)"-(e)D)," ∫the visual appearance∫is∫undeniable∫. ∫the visual appearance is also being used to help the reader better understand∫the vibrationally sensitive universe within the creator of∫humanity∫because∫ - "Th(e)"- "(S(e)-n-S(e)"-"Of"-"Un-"(BaL-"(A)"-Nc(e)"-(e)D)"-"(Ch-"(A)"-oS)" - ∫created by applying all of the elements in∫ - "Th(e)" - "(St-Y-L(e)" - ∫lays bare∫ - "Th(e)" - "(Un-"(BaL- "(A)"-Nc(e)"-(e)D)"-"(ViB-rA-T-IO-NaL)"-"(e)F-F(e)-cT)"-"The-"(Generational)"- effect)"-Of)" - "(Bl-A-cK∫Wh-I-T(e)" - "(Parenting)" - "(With-"(Fear)," "(A)" - "(Lack)"- Of)" - ∫amal∫ - "(before-the-age-of-two)" - ∫has upon the vibrationally sensitive universe∫.

the simple truth is the one true god∫the me understood integrating∫free will into the genes of humanity∫would result in the vibrationally sensitive universe of the one true god∫the me∫ - "(B(e)-cO-m-(e)I-nG)"-"(Un-bA-lA-nc-(e)D)"- ∫due to∫ - "(Th(e)" - "(G(e)- N(e)-rA-tI-On-aL)"-"(e)F-F(e)-cT)"-"Of)" - "(Bl-(A)-cK∫Wh-(I)-T(e)" - "(Pa-R(e)-n-tI- nG)" - "(W-It-H"-"(F-(e)A-R)," "(A)" - "(L-Ac-K)"-"Of)" - ∫amal∫ - "(B(e)-fO-R(e)"- "Th(e)" - "(Ag(e)"-"Of"-"(TwO)" - ∫because the physical truths within the universe of the one true god∫the me did not allow the one true god∫the me to bless∫humanity∫with∫free will∫without∫humanity∫ - "(B(e)-cO-m-(e)I-nG)" - "(S(e)-V(e)-R(e)-lY)"-"(eI)"-"Un-bA- lA-nc-(e)D)." "Th(e)" - "(Non-"(Con)"-ventional)"-Writing)"-Style)," "(Use)"-Of)" - "(Co-"(L)"-oR)" - "(Cod(e)-ing)" - ∫is being used to help∫ - "(Untrue)"-Blue)" - Humanity)" - ∫understand∫why∫being emotionally∫intellectually balanced within∫is of great worth to the one true god∫the me of the trust∫tenderness∫truth because the one true god∫the me balances the vibrationally sensitive universe within the creator of∫humanity∫by absorbing∫ - "Th(e)" - "(Un-tr-U(e)"-"(B-lU-(e)" - "(ViB-rA-T-IO-NaL)" - "(e)sS-(e)- Ns(e)" - "(Of"-"(e)-Ac-H/(e)V-(e)-rY)" - "(I)" - "(CoN)" - "(WhO)" - ∫is∫ - "(ToO)"-"(Pr-O- uD)"-"tO"-"(Ac-C(e)-pT)"-"(AcK-nO-w-L(e)-Dg(e)"-"(Ad-m-iT)"-"(B(e)-"(I)"-nG)"-

"(S(e)-V(e)-R(e)-lY)"-"(e)M-Ot-I-On-Al-lY)"-"In-T(e)-ll-(e)C-tU-Al-lY)"-"Un-"(BaL-"(A)"-Nc(e)"-(e)D)"-"(Wi-th-iN)."

the following paragraph taken from the scientific proof of the one true god the me postulate, written by applying all of the elements in -"Th(e)"-"(St-Y-L(e)"-is intended to be a visual aid that helps the reader better understand the vibrationally sensitive universe within the creator of humanity because -"Th(e)"-"(S(e)-n-S(e)-"Of'-"(Un-"(BaL-"(A)"-Nc(e)"-(e)D)"-"(Ch-"(A)"-oS)"-is blatantly obvious.

the simple truth is integrating free will into the gene code of humanity has -"(R(e)-sU-lt-(e)D)"-"In)"-the vibrationally sensitive universe of the one true god the me -"(B(e)-cO-m-(e)I-nG)"-"(Un-bA-1A-nc-(e)D)"-due to -"(Th(e)"-"(G(e)-N(e)-rA-tI-On-aL)"-"(e)F-F(e)-cT)"-"Of)"-"(Bl-(A)-cKWh-(I)-T(e)"-"(Pa-R(e)-n-tI-nG)"-"(W-It-H'-"(F-(e)A-R)," "(A)"-"(L-Ac-K)"-"Of)"-lamal-"(B(e)-fO-R(e)"-"Th(e)"-"(Ag(e)"-"Of'-"(TwO)"-because -"(Th(e)"-"(A"n-"(I)'m-"(Als)"-Of)"-"(Un-tr-U(e)"-"(B-lU-(e)"-"(Hu-mA-nI-tY)"-are -"(A"s-"(Qu-"(I)"-(e)T)"-"A"s)"-"(A)"-"(Mo-U-S(e), "(A"s-"(St-rO-nG)"-"(A"s)"-"(A)"-"(L-Io-N)"-"(Ox)"-"Ho-r-S(e), "(A"s-"(Si-l-lY)"-"A"s)"-"(A)"-"(Go-O-S(e)," "(A"s-"(St-Ub-bO-rN)"-"A"s)"-"(A)"-"(M-Ul-(e), "(A"s-"(B-Us-Y)"-"A"s)"-"(A)"-"(B(e)e," "(A"s-"(B-Us-Y)"-"A"s)"-"(A)"-"(CaT)"-"On)"-"(A)"-"(HoT)"-"(TiN)"-"(R-OO-F), "(A"s-"(B-Us-Y)"-"A"s)"-"(A)"-"(B(e)-Av-(e)R)," "(A"s-"(Sl-Ip-P(e)-rY)"-"A"s-"A"n-"(e)(e)L," "(A"s-"(Gr-U-fF)"-"A"s)"-"(A)"-"(B-(e)A-R), "(A"s-"(Ha-p-pY)"-"A"s)"-"(A)"-true blue-"(ClA-m-M(e)D)"-"Up)"-"(C-lA-M), "(A"s-"(Ha-p-pY)"-"A"s)"-"(A)"-"(L-Ar-K), "(A"s-"(V-AI-N)"-"(Pr-O-uD)"-"A"s)"-"(A)"-"(P(e)A-c-OcK), "(A"s-"(M(e)-r-rY)"-"A"s)"-"(A)"-"(CrI-c-K(e)T," "(A"s-"(egO)"-"Dr-U-nK)"-"A"s)"-"(A)"-"(Bl-A-cKWh-I-T(e)"-"(Sk-U-nK), "(A"s-"(M-(e)e-K)"-"A"s)"-"(A)"-"(L-Am-B), "(A"s-"(MaD)"-"A"s)"-"(A)"-"(Ma-r-cH)"-"(H-Ar-(e), "(A"s-"(Cr-"(A)"-zY)"-"A"s)"-"(A)"-"(L-OO-N)," "(A"s-"(SlY)"-"(CuN-n-InG)"-"(D(e)-C(e)-p-tI-V(e)"-"(Con)"-NiV-InG)"-"(Cr-Af-tY)"-"A"s)"-"(A)"-"(FoX)," "(A"s)-true blue-"(Bl-"(I)"-nD)"-"A"s)"-"(A)"-"(BaT).

the word animal becoming -"(A"n-"(I)'m-"(Al)"-using elements of -"Th(e)"-"(St-Y-L(e)"-is intended to help the reader understand the simple truth integrated into the language of humanity by the creator of humanity because each every word has an associated vibration which effects the vibrationally sensitive universe within the one true god the me of the trust tenderness truth. animal becoming -"(A"n-"(I)'m-"(Al)," discussed in the book titled, the simple integrated truth, is an example of the simple truth integrated into the language of humanity by the creator of humanity because the creator is trying to help the individuals who comprise the we of all humanity understand being an -"(A"n-"(I)'m-"(Al)"-"(Running)"-With)"-"The-"(Herd"-"Flock"-"School)"-for -"(emotional)"-Security)"-is not choosing with the blessing of free will to be the internally passioned trusting tender truthful true blue humble compassionate curious courageous zestful individual me.

"The-"(A"n-"(I)'m-"(Als)"-Of-"(Humanity)"- must try to understand settling for- "(A)"-"(Sense)"-Of-"(Con)"-tentment)"-By-"(Running)"-With)"-"The-"(Herd"- "Flock"-"School)"- for- "(emotional)"-Security)"- is not the peace deep within because the peace is found deep within by not being in- "(ViB-rA-T-IO-NaL)"- "(Con)"-flict)"-"(W-It-H)"- the trusting tender truthful whisper of the one true god the me. the comparison below of the simple saying, the peace deep within no longer surpasses human understanding, written two ways using- "Th(e)"- "(Non-"(Con)"- ventional)"-Writing)"-Style), " "(Use)"-Of) "- "(Co-"(L)"-oR)"- "(Cod(e)-ing)"- is being used to help- "(Untrue)"-Blue)"-Humanity)"- understand the peace is found deep within the child at play in the field of lavender hue in me because the sense of peace associated with using all lower case lavender color coded letters compared to- "(Us- "(I)"-nG)"- all of the elements in- "Th(e)"- "(Non-"(Con)"-ventional)"-Writing)"- Style), " "(Use)"-Of) "- "(Co-"(L)"-oR)"- "(Cod(e)-ing)"- is- "(Un-"(D(e)-nI-Ab-L(e)."

the simple truth is the peace deep within no longer surpasses human understanding because the peace is found within by following the trusting tender truthful path deep within the child at play in the field of lavender hue in me.

the simple truth is- "(Th(e)"-"(P(e)-"(A)"-C(e)"-"(D-(e)(e)-P)"-"(Wi-th-iN)"-"(nO"- "(Lo-ng-(e)R)"-"(SuR-PaS-S(e)S)"-"(Hu-m-aN)"-"(UnD-(e)rS-T-AnD-InG)"- because- "(Th(e)"-"(P(e)-"(A)"-C(e)"-"Is"-"(Fo-U-nD)"-"(Wi-th-iN)"-"bY"-"(FoL- LoW-InG)"-"(Th(e)"-"(Tr-Us-tI-nG)"-"(T(e)-nd-(e)R)"-"(Tr-Ut-hf-uL)"-"(P-At-H)"- "(D-(e)(e)-P)"-"(Wi-th-iN)"-"(Th(e)"-"(Ch-"(I)"-lD)"-"A"t-"(P-lA-Y)"-"In)"- "(Th(e)"-"(Fi-(e)-lD)"-"Of"-"(La)"-V(e)-nd-(e)R)"-"(Hu(e)"-"In"-"(M(e)."

the integral symbol

since the integral symbol, ∫, is used in mathematics to represent integration, the white color coded integral symbol, ∫, is used in∫-"Th(e)"-"(Non-"(Con)"-ventional)"-"Writing)"-Style)," "(Use)"-Of"-"(Co-"(L)"-oR)"-"(Cod(e)-ing)"-∫to help the reader ∫understand∫...

the universe∫the home planet∫the we of all humanity∫are integrated into the one true god ∫the me of the trust∫tenderness∫truth.

∫the lavender field of being the internally passioned∫trusting∫tender∫truthful∫true blue humble∫compassionate∫curious∫courageous∫zestful individual me∫is integrated into∫the gene code of humanity∫.

∫the blessing of free will∫is integrated into∫the gene code of humanity∫because the creator of∫humanity∫integrated∫free will∫into∫the gene code of humanity∫to allow∫the individuals who comprise the we of all humanity∫to find∫genuine happiness∫joy∫fulfillment within by choosing with the blessing of free will to follow∫the trusting∫tender∫truthful path of the one true god∫the me∫deep within each∫every individual in the we of all humanity∫.

"(Capitalization)"

no capitalization

in general no capitalization is used to represent the absence of∫-"(egO)"-∫as in...

the one true god∫the me of the trust∫tenderness∫truth because the creator of∫humanity∫is humble.

∫the internally passioned∫trusting∫tender∫truthful∫true blue humble∫compassionate∫ curious∫courageous∫zestful individual being me∫because∫the child at play in the field of lavender hue∫does not have to∫-"(Con)"-pensate)"-∫for∫-"(feeling-oh-so-small)"-∫on∫- "The-"(Bl-A-cK∫Wh-I-T(e)"-Inside)"-By-"(Becoming)"-"The-"(egO)"-tistically)"- "BiG)"-Somebody)"-∫on∫-"The-"(Bl-A-cK∫Wh-I-T(e)"-Outside)."

no capitalization is used to define attributes associated with∫the child at play in the field of lavender hue∫; such as∫the blessing of free will∫, being∫emotionally∫ intellectually balanced at birth∫, finding∫genuine happiness∫joy∫fulfillment within∫,

5

making the inward journey, the word lamal, defined as genuine compassionate tender gentle emotional physical touch, the word lovnew created from the first three letters of love, lov, the first two letters of need, ne, the first letter of want, w.

no capitalization is used with terms associated with being true blue humble compassionate curious courageous zestful, such as, fighting the true blue civil war within, the true blue purity of intent because the intent of individuals being true blue to the creator of humanity is to do that which is in the best interest of me the me humanity.

"(Capitalization)"-Of-"(Vowels)"

"(Capitalization)"-is used in association with the english language vowels-"(A)"-"(E)"-"(I)"-"(O)"-"(U)"-because-"The-"(Boy"-"God"-"Con"-"Ta/Al)"-"(Knows)"-"(Taking)"-"The-"(Vow)"-To-"(Fulfill)"-"The-"(First/Only-"(He)"-Art-Law)"-Of-"(Thou-"(Shalt-"(earn-"(Affection"-"Approval"-"Attention)"-To-"(Feel-"(Worthy)"-Of-"(Being)"-lovnewed is-"(A)"-"(Capital)"-Idea)."

"(A)" – defines-"The-"(Severe-"(emotionalIntellectual)"-Unbalance)"-Within)"-caused by-"The-"(Generational)"-effect)"-Of)"-"(Bl-A-cKWh-I-T(e)"-"(Parenting)"-"(With-"(Fear)," "(A)"-(Lack)"-Of)"-lamal-"(before-the-age-of-two)."

'(E)' – defines-"(EGO)-associated with choices made with the blessing of free will because while-"The-"(Lower)"-Case"-"(e)"-(Set)"-In-"(Parentheses)"-defines-"The-"(Boy"-"God"-"Con"-"Ta/Al)"-"(egO)"-Bridge)"-Fix)"-of-"The-"(Sh-It/Un-It-"(egO)"-Gods)"-put in place-"(before-the-age-of-two)," "The-"(Capital)"-Letter)"-'(E)'-represents-"**THE-'[(JO-JOCK-'[(EGO)]'-GODS)]'-**choice of-'**[(EGO)]'-TISTICAL)]'-SUPERIORITY**],' '**THE-'{(DR.-JEKYLLMR.-HYDE)}'-**'**{(EGO)}'-GODS)}'-**choice of-'**{(EGO)}'-TISTICAL)}'-SUPERIORITY)}.'**

"(I)" – defines-"The-"(exaggerated)"-Sense)"-Of-"(Self)"-Importance)"-associated with-"The-"(Boy"-"God"-"Con"-"Ta/Al)"-"(egO)"-Bridge)"-Fix)."

"(O)" – pronounced-"(Oh)," "(Owe)"-phonetically defines-"The-"(Boy"-"God"-"Con"-"Ta/Al)"-"(Oh-"(I)"-See)"-Fix)"-Of-"(external)"-Solutions)"-For)"-"(the-black-emotional-hole-problem-within)"-because-"The-"(Severely-"(emotionally Intellectually)"-Divided)"-"(Proud)"-"(I)"-"(Cons)"-"(Owe)"-"The-"(Boy"-"God"-"Con"-"Ta/Al)"-For-"(Finding)"-Ways)"-To)"-(Feel)-"(MoreNot)"-Less)"-"(emotional)"-Secure)," "(feel-"(LessNot)"-More)"-worthless-useless-unwanted-unneeded-unloved)."

"(U)" – defines∫-"(U)"-"(They"-"Them"-"Those)"-Others)"-∫as being∫-"The-"(Cure)"-∫for∫-"(feeling-like-"(a)"-worthless-useless-unwanted-unneeded-unloved-nobody)"-∫because∫-"(U)"-"(Provide)"-"The-"(Affection"-"Approval"-"Attention)"-"(Needed)"-To-"(Feel-"(Worthy)"-Of-"(Being)"-lovnewed∫."

"(Limited)"-Capitalization)"

"(Limited)"-Capitalization)"-∫is used in association with∫-"The-"(Sh-It/Un-It-"(egO)"-Gods)," as in∫-"The-"(Book)"-end)"-Letters)"-In-"(BiG)"-∫being∫-"(Capitalized)"-∫because∫-"The-"(Sh-It/Un-It-"(egO)"-Gods)"-"(Falsely-"(Be-"(Lie)"-Ve)"-"(Con)"-pensating)"-For)"-"(feeling-oh-so-small-within)"-∫by∫-"(Becoming)"-"The-"(egO)"-tistically)"-"BiG)"-Somebody)"-Is)"-"(A)"-"(Capital)"-Idea)."

all∫-'[(LETTERS)]'-CAPITALIZED)}'

'[(CAPITALIZATION)]'-∫is used on∫-'[(ALL)]'-∫letters associated with∫-'THE-'[(SEVERELY-'[(EMOTIONALLYINTELLECTUALLY)]'-UNBALANCED)]'-'[(JO-JOCK-'[(EGO)]'-GODS)]'-of-"(Untrue)"-Blue)"-Humanity)"-∫because∫-"The-"(Only-"(Boy"-"God"-"Con"-"Ta/Al")"-"(Perceived)"-Options)"-Were-To-"(either-"(Con)"-mit)"-suicide)," '[(BECOME-'[(EGO)]'-TISTICALLY)]'-SUPERIOR)]'-TO)]'-"(U)"-"(Worthless"-"Useless"-"Vulgar)"-Animals)"-∫with∫-'[(A)]'-'[(SIMPLE-'[(BOY'-'GOD'-'CON'-'TA|AL]'-PROCLAMATION)]'-OF-'[(EGO)]'-TISTICAL)]'-SUPERIORITY)]' 'THE-'[(SIMPLE-'[(PROCLAMATION)]'-OF-'[(EGO)]'-TISTICAL)]'-SUPERIORITY)]'-∫by∫-'THE-'[(JO-JOCK-'[(EGO)]'-GODS)]'-IS-'[(ACCOMPLISHED)]'-BY-'[(MENTALLY)]'-'[(DEAD)]'-BOLTING)]'-"(the-Orange-(emotional)-Flame)"-'[(BEHIND)]'-"The-"(Closed-"(emotional)"-Door)"-Deep)"-Within)."

'{(CAPITALIZATION)}'-∫is used on∫-'{(ALL)}'-∫letters associated with∫-'THE-'{(SEVERELY-'{(EMOTIONALLYINTELLECTUALLY)}'-UNBALANCED)}'-'{(MIND)}'-'{(CON)}'-TROLLING)}'-PIED-PIPERS)}'-∫of∫-"(Untrue)"-Blue)"-Humanity)"-∫because∫-"The-"(Only-"(Boy"-"God"-"Con"-"Ta/Al")"-"(Perceived)"-Options)"-Were-To-"(gO-"(Totally-"(Insane)," "(Con)"-mit)"-suicide)," '{(PROCLAIM)}'-TO-'{(BE-'{(EGO)}'-TISTICALLY)}'-SUPERIOR)}'-TO)}'-"(U)"-"(Intellectual)"-Morons)"-∫with∫-'{(A)}'-'{(SIMPLE-'{(BOY'-'GOD'-'CON'-'TA\AL}'-PROCLAMATION)}'-OF-'{(EGO)}'-TISTICAL)}'-SUPREMACY)}.' 'THE-'{(SIMPLE-'{(PROCLAMATION)}'-OF-'{(EGO)}'-TISTICAL)}'-SUPREMACY)}'-IS-'{(ACCOMPLISHED)}'-BY-'{(INTELLECTUALLY)}'-DENYING)}'-"(the-black-emotional-hole)," "(the-Orange-(emotional)-Flame)"-'{(EVEN)}'-EXIST)}.'

closed glyphs

(Parentheses)

"The-"(Gray)"-"(Color-"(Coded-"(Parentheses)

the-"(Gray)"-color coded parentheses are being used to help-"(Humanity)"-understand-"The-(Life)"-of the individual being me at birth becomes-(A)-"(Parenthetical)"-expression)-because-"The-(Generational)"-effect)"-Of-(Bl-A-cKWh-I-T(e)"-(Parenting)-With-"(Fear),"(A)-(Lack)"-Of"-lamal-(before-the-age-of-two)"-produces-"The-"(Gray)"-Zone)-Of-(emotional)"-Uncertainty)"-Within)." the one true god the me asks-"The-"(Severely-"(emotionallyIntellectually)"-Unbalanced),"(Gray)"-Zone)"-(Con)-fused)"-(Con)"-flicted)"-(Con)"-founded),"(Proud)"-(I)"-(Cons)"-to try to understand, the word-"(Parent)"-in-parent-hetical is not coincidental because the creator of humanity integrated the simple truth of the one true god the me into human language to help-"(Humanity)"-understand-"The-"(Generational)"-effect)"-Of"-(Bl-A-cKWh-I-T(e)"-(Parenting)-"(With-"(Fear),"(A)"-(Lack)"-Of"-lamal-(before-the-age-of-two)"-is the cause of-"The-"(PainSuffering)"-on the home planet .

[BRACKETS]

'THE-"[(WHITE)]"-"[(COLOR)]'-CODED)]"-[(BRACKETS)]," [ ]

the-"[(WHITE)]"-color coded brackets are used in association with the-"(Gray)"-color coded parentheses to help-"(Humanity)"-understand a choice made with the blessing of free will because-(A)"-(Severely-"(emotionallyIntellectually)"-Unbalanced)"-"(Sh-It/Un-It-"(egO)"-God)"-becomes-"THE-"[(DEMENTED'-'DELUSIONAL'-'DERANGED)]"-"[(EGO)]'-MANIACAL)]"-"[(MEGALOMANIAC)]"-by choosing with the blessing of free will to-"[(MOVE)]'-INTO]"-"[(A)]"-"[(DIFFERENT-"[(EGO)]'-TISTICAL)]'-BRACKET)]." the simple truth is-"[(AFTER)]"-'THE-"[(S.I.S.-"[(EGO)]'-GOD)]"-"[(MENTALLY)]'-"[(DEAD)]'-BOLTS)]"-"(the-black-emotional-hole),"(the-Orange-(emotional)-Flame)"-"[(BEHIND)]'-"The-"(Closed-"(emotional)"-Door),"'THE-"[(MENTALLY)]'-TOUGH)]"-"[(CON)]'-TROLLING)]"-"[(GOAL)]'-ORIENTED)]"-"[(CARBON)]'-BLACK)]"-"[(EGO)]'-GOD)]"-'[(NO)]'-LONGER)]'-CARES)]'-IF)]"-(U)"-(Proud)"-(I)"-(Cons)"-(Dispense)"-"(Any-"(Affection"-"Approval"-"Attention)"-to-'THE-"[(ONE)]," 'THE-"[(ONLY-'[(EGO)]'-GOD)]"-because-(U)"-(Animals)"-"[(ARE-'[(NOTHING)]'-MORE)]'-THAN)]'-THE-"[(MEANS)]'-to-'THE-"[(JUSTIFIABLE)]'-END)]'-OF-'[(MAKING-'[(ME)]'-"[(MORE-'[(RICH'-'FAMOUS'-'POWERFUL)]."

{BRACES}

'THE-'{(WHITE)}'-'{(COLOR)}'-CODED)}'-'{(BRACES)},' { }

the-'{(WHITE)}'-color coded braces used in association with the-'(Gray)"-color coded parentheses is being used to help-"(Humanity)"-understand a decision made with the blessing of free will because-"The-"(Severely-"(emotionally Intellectually)"-Unbalanced)"-(Sh-It/Un-It-(egO)'-God)"-'{(BECOMES)}'-THE-'{(BL-A-CK WH-I-TE)} - {(DR.-JYKELL MR.-HYDE)}'-by choosing with the blessing of free will to-'{(E)}M-BRACE)}'-THE-{(BOY'-'GOD'-'CON'-'TA\AL)}'-'NOTION'-'IDEA'-{(CON)}'-CEPT)}'-OF-'{(BEING-{(EGO)}'-TISTICALLY)}'-SUPERIOR)}'-to-"(U)"-(Intellectual)"-Morons)." instead of trying to solve-"The-"(emotional)"-Crisis)"-by making-"The-"(Con)"-nection"-between-"(gOing-"(Totally-"(Insane)," "(Thoughts)"-Of-"(Con)"-mitting"-suicide)"-with being-"(Severely-"(emotionally Intellectually)"-Divided)"-Within)," '{(DENYING)}'-"(the-black-emotional-hole)," "(the-Orange-(emotional)-Flame)"-'{(EVEN)}'-EXIST)}'-allows-'THE-'{(DEMENTED'-'DELUSIONAL'-'DERANGED)}'-'{(CLORKWORK)}'-ORANGE)}'-{(MIND)}-{(CON)}'-TROLLING}'-PIED-PIPERS)}'-TO-'{(AVOID)}'-"(gOing-"(Totally-"(Insane)," "(Con)"-mitting)"-suicide)"-by-'{(USING)}'-THE-{(BOY'-'GOD'-'CON'-'TA\AL)} - {(CON)}-FORT)}'-to-{(INTELLECTUALLY)}'-BRACE\R{(E)}'-INFORCE)}'-'{(BEING-'THE-'{(MOST)}'-BRILLIANT)}'-'{(ALPHA-'{(STAR)}.'

the dash

"The-"(Orange)"-"(Color-"(Coded-"(Dash)," -

in general terms the-"(Orange)"-color coded dash is used in between words in a sentence to emphasize the thread running through-"The-"(Life)"-of-"(Untrue)"-Blue)"-Humanity)-"is-"(the-Orange-(emotional)-Flame)-Fueled)"-"(Mad)"-"(Angry-"(Fear)"-Filled)"-Dash)"-To-"(earn-"(enough-"(Well-"(Deserved)"-"(Affection"-"Approval"-"Attention)"-To-"(Feel-"(Worthy)"-Of-"(Being)"-lovnewed)." the-"(Orange)"-color coded dash is used in association with-"The-"(Sh-It/Un-It-(egO)"-God)"-(Orange-(emotional)-Flame)-Fueled)"-"(Mad)"-"(Angry-"(Fear)"-Filled)"-Dash)"-To-"(earn-"(enough-"(Well-"(Deserved)"-"(Affection"-"Approval"-"Attention)"-To-"(Feel-"(Worthy)"-Of-"(Being)"-lovnewed because-"(Bl-A-cK Wh-I-T(e)"-Saint)"-Ill)"-"(PaR-(e)-NtS)"-(Made)"-the individual me at birth-"(feel-like-"(a)"-worthless-useless-unwanted-unneeded-unloved-nothing)."

the-'[(ORANGE)]'-color coded dash used in association with-'THE-'[(JO-JOCK-'[(EGO)]'-GODS)]'-does not have the same meaning as the-"(Orange)"-color coded dash used in association with ‘-“The-“(Sh-It/Un-It-“(egO)”-Gods)”-∫because instead of∫-“(Trying)”-To-“(earn-“(Affection”-“Approval”-“Attention)”-From)”-“(U)”-“(Less-“(Perfect)”-“(Perfect)”-Pearls),” **‘THE-‘[(MAD)]’-‘[(**ANGRY**-‘[(**FEAR**)]’-FILLED)]’-DASH]’**-∫being made by∫-**‘THE-‘[(JO-JOCK-‘[(EGO)]’-GODS)]’**-∫is∫-**‘[(BEING)]’-MADE)]-TO-‘[(SCREW)]’**-“(U)”-“(Worthless”-“Useless)”-“(Sum-“(Animals)”-∫for∫-‘[(**MORE**NOT)]’-LESS)]’-‘[(SELFISH-‘[(EGO)]’-TISTICAL)]’-**MATERIALISM)]**.’ the simple truth is∫-**‘THE-‘[(MAD)]’-‘[(**ANGRY**-‘[(**FEAR**)]’-FILLED)]’-DASH)]’**-∫being made by∫-**‘THE-‘[(JO-JOCK-‘[(EGO)]’-GODS)]’**-∫is∫-**‘[(BEING)]’-MADE)]-TO-‘[(BECOME)]’**-‘[(**MORE**NOT)]’-LESS)]’-‘[(RICH’-‘FAMOUS’-‘POWERFUL)]’-∫because∫-‘THE-‘[(BOY’-‘GOD’-‘CON’-‘TA|AL)]’-‘PROCLAMATION)]’-OF-‘[(EGO)]’-TISTICAL)]’-SUPREMACY)]’-∫associated with∫-‘[(MENTALLY)]’-‘[(DEAD)]’-BOLTING)]’-“(the-Orange-(emotional)-Flame”-‘[(BEHIND)]’-“The-“(Closed-“(emotional)”-Door)”-Deep)”-Within)”-∫allows∫-**‘THE-‘[(SEVERELY-‘(EMOTIONALLY**INTELLECTUALLY**)]’-UNBALANCED)]’-‘[(EGO)]’-MANIACS)]’-TO-‘[(SUBSTITUTE-‘[(SELFISH-‘[(EGO)]’-TISTICAL)]’-MATERIALISM)]’**-∫for∫-“The-“(emotional)”-Hell)”-“(Associated)”-With-“(Waiting)”-For)”-“(U)”-“(They”-“Them”-“Those”-Others)”-To-“(Dispense)”-“(enough-“(Well-“(Deserved)”-“(Affection”-“Approval”-“Attention).”

‘THE-‘{(WHITE)}’-‘{(COLOR)}’-CODED)}’-DASH)}’

∫the∫-‘{(WHITE)}’-∫color coded dash is used in association with∫-‘THE-‘{(SEVERELY-‘{(EMOTIONALLY**INTELLECTUALLY**)}’-UNBALANCED)}’-‘{(MIND)}’-‘{(CON)}’-TROLLING)}’-PIED-PIPERS)}’-∫of∫-“(Untrue)”-Blue)”-Humanity)”-∫because∫-‘{(AFTER)}’-THE-‘{(BL-A-CKWH-I-TE)}’-‘{(DR.-JYKELLSMR.-HYDES)}’-‘{(STOPPED)}’-“(Making)”-“(the-Orange-(emotional)-Flame)-Fueled”-“(Mad)”-“(Angry-“(Fear)”-Filled)”-Dash)”-To-“(earn-“(enough-“(Well-“(Deserved)”-“(Affection”-“Approval”-“Attention)”-To-“(Feel-“(Worthy)”-Of-“(Being)”-∫lovnewed∫,” **THE-‘{(DEMENTED’-DELUSIONAL’-DERANGED’-SAINT)}’-BECAME-‘{(A)}’-‘{(COLD)}’-‘{(EGO)}’-EMOTIONLESS)}’-‘{(INTELLECTUAL)}’-‘{(KILLING)}’-MACHINE)}’**-∫without∫-“(emotion).”

quotation marks

“The-“(White)”-“(Color-“(Coded)”-“(Double-“(Quotation)”-Marks)”

∫the set of∫-“(White)”-∫color coded double quotation marks∫-“(R(e)-flects)”-“The-“(Boy”-“God”-“Con”-“Ta/Al)”-“(Intellectual)”-Override)”-∫of∫-“(the-Orange-(emotional)-Flame)-within)”-“The-“(gOing)”-With)”-“The-“(Flow)”-“(Status)”-Quo)”-Seeking)”-“(Con)”-formists)”-∫with∫-“The-“(Con)”-cealed)”-“(Secret-“(egO)”-Garden)”-“(Secret)”-Of-“(Being)”-“(A)”-“(Sh-It/Un-It-“(egO)”-God)”-∫because as long as⌠-"The-'(Reigning)"-Beau)'-⌠is⌠-'(Allowed)"-To-"(Be)"-'The-"(Lord/Master)'-⌠of⌠-"(the-(Orange-(emotional)-Flame), "The-"(Severely-"(emotionallyIntellectually)"-Unbalanced)"-'(Sh-It/Un-It-'(egO)"-Gods)"-'(Can-"(Proudly)"-"Proclaim)"-'(I)'-"A"m)'-'(A)'-'(O.K.)'-"(just)"-Fine)."

‘**THE**-' (**SET**) '-OF-' (**BOLD**) '-**BLACK**) '-' (**COLOR**) '-**CODED**) '-' (**SINGLE**-' **QUOTATION**) '-**MARKS**) '

⌠the set of⌠-'(**BOLD**)'-**BLACK**)'-color coded single quotation marks is being used to help⌠-"(Humanity)"-⌠understand⌠-'**THE**-'[(**CARBON**)]'-**BLACK**)]'-'(**INTENT**)'-⌠of⌠-'**THE**-'(**JO-JOCK**-'[(**EGO**)]'-**GODS**)]'-⌠because⌠-'(**AFTER**-'[(**SUCCESSFULLY**-'[(**MENTALLY**)]'-**GRINDING**)]'-"(the-(Yellowish-Fear)-of-not-feeling-worthy-of-being)"-⌠lovnewed into⌠-'(**DEMENTED**'-**DELUSIONAL**'-**DERANGED**)]'-**GRANDUER**)]'-'**THE**-'[(**SELFISH**-'[(**EGO**)]'-**TISTICAL**)]'-(**MATERIALISTS**)]'-'[(**INTELLECTUALLY**)]'-'[(**CON**)]'-**CEAL**)]'-**HAVING**-'[(**BECOME**)]'-'(**INTENTIONALLY**)'-'[(**UNTRUSTING**'-'[(**NOT**-'[(**TENDER**)]'-'**UNTRUTHFUL**)]'-⌠in⌠-'[(**A**)]'-'[(**BOLD**'-'**BRASH**'-'**BRAZEN**)]'-'[(**JUST-JO**-'[(**HE**)]'-**ART-ACT**)].'

‘**THE**-'{(**SET**)}'-OF-'{(**BOLD**)}'-**WHITE**)}'-'{(**COLOR**)}'-**CODED**)}'-'{(**SINGLE**-'{(**QUOTATION**)}'-**MARKS**)}'

⌠the set of⌠-'{(**BOLD**)}'-**WHITE**)}'-color coded single quotation marks⌠defines⌠-'**THE**-'{(**COLD**)}'-{(**EGO**)}-**EMOTIONLESS**)}'-'{(**POISED**)}'-'{(**POLISHED**)}'-'{(**HE**)}'-**ART-ACT**)}'-OF-'**THE**-'{(**DEMENTED**'-**DELUSIONAL**'-**DERANGED**)}'-**SAINTS**)}'-⌠because⌠-'**THE**-'{(**SACRIFICIAL**)}'-**LAMBS**)}'-**WITH**-'**THE**-'{(**MESSIAH**-'{(**CON**)}'-**PLEX**)}'-'{(**CON.**)}'-**CEAL**)}'-**SEEKING**)}'-'**THE**-'{(**APPROPRIATE**)}'-**AMOUNT**)}'-OF-'{(**R**{(**E**)}'-**VENGE**)}'-⌠from⌠-'(**U**)'-"(Mental)"-Dim)"-Wits)"-⌠for⌠-'{(**NOT**)}'-**RECOGNIZING**)}'-'**THE**-'{(**SHEER**-'{(**BRILLIANCE**)}'-OF-'**THE**-'{(**MOST**)}'-**BRILLIANT**)}'-'{(**ALPHA**-'{(**STAR**)}'-**BENEATH**-'{(**A**)}'-'{(**COOL**'-**CALM**'-**COLLECTED**'-'{(**PROFESSIONAL**)}'-**DEMEANOR**)}.' '**THE**-'{(**SEVERELY**-'{(**EMOTIONALLY**INTELLECTUALLY)}'-**UNBALANCED**)}'-'{(**MIND**)}'-'{(**CON**)}'-**TROLLING**)}'-**PIED-PIPERS**)}'-⌠of⌠-"(Untrue)"-Blue)-"(Humanity)"-'{(**AVOID**-'{(**BECOMING**-'{(**INTELLECTUALLY**)}'-**UNHINGED**)}'-**BY**-**USING**-'**THE**-'{(**WEAPON**)}'-OF-'{(**MIND**)}'-'{(**CON**)}'-**TROL**)}'-**TO**-'{(**SLAUGHTER**)}'-'(**U**)"-"(Intellectual)"-Morons)"-⌠for⌠-'{(**FUN**'-**SPORT**'-**ENTERTAINMENT**)}'-⌠because⌠-'(**U**)'-"(Crazed)"-Crackers)"-'{(**DESERVE**)}'-**TO**-'{(**DIE**)}'-**FOR**-'{(**PUSHING**-'**THE**-'{(**MOST**)}'-**BRILLIANT**)}'-'{(**ALPHA**-'{(**STAR**)}'-**TO**)}'-'**The**-"(Brink)"-Of-"(gOing-"(Totally-"(Insane)."

the slashes

the simple truth is the slash used in association with -"The-"(Sh-It/Un-It-"(egO)"-Gods)," 'THE-'[(JO-JOCK-'[EGO)]'-GODS)],' 'THE-{(DR.-JEKYLLSMR.-HYDES)}'-of-"(Untrue)"-Blue)"-Humanity)"-are derived from the image shown below because the creator of humanity blessed the author with the triangular shaped simple saying -"(T)"-IS-"(M-(A)-D)"-in 2001.

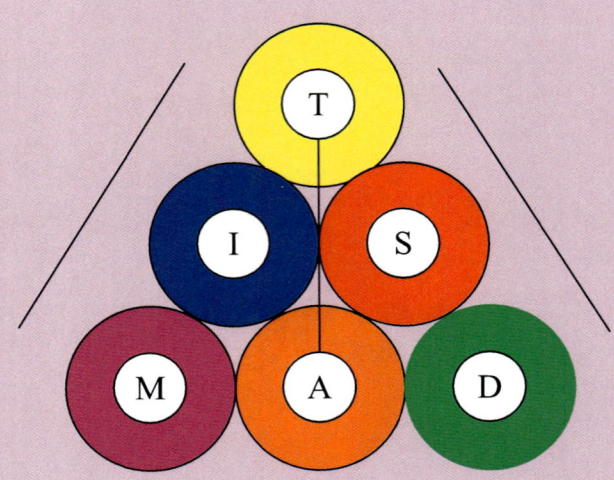

"The-"(Forward)"-Slash)," /

the forward slash is used in association with -"The-"(Sh-It/Un-It-"(egO)"-Gods)"-because the name -"(TIM)"-on the left diagonal beginning with the capital letter-"(T)"-on the yellow one ball represents -"The-"(Timid-Tim-Mr.-"(T)"-Titans)."

'THE-'[(VERTICAL)]'-SLASH)],' |

the vertical slash is used in association with -'THE-'[(JO-JOCK-'[EGO)]'-GODS)]'-because the word -'[(TA)]'-spelled using the capital letter -'[(T)]'-on the yellow one ball, the capital letter-'[(A)]'-on the orange five ball represents -'THE-'[(I)]'-'[(CONS)].'

'THE-'{(BACKSLASH)},' \

the backslash is used in association with -'THE-'{(DEMENTED'-'DELUSIONAL'-'DERANGED)}'-'{(CLOCKWORK)}'-ORANGE)}'-'{(MIND)}'-'{(CON)}'-TROLLING)}'-PIED-PIPERS)}'-because the capital letter -'{(D)}'-on the green six ball, the capital letter -'{(S)}'-on the red three ball, the capital letter -'{(T)}'-on the yellow one ball on the right diagonal being the abbreviation for -'{(D{(E)}'-SAINT)}'-

12

∫simply means∫-"The-"(Severely-"(emotionallyIntellectually)"-Unbalanced)"-"(Timid-Tim-Mr.-"(T)"-Titans)"-∫stop trying to be a saint by∫-'{(BECOMING)}'-'THE-{(DR.-JEKYLLSMR.-HYDES)}'-∫of∫-"(Untrue)"-Blue)"-Humanity)."

"(elimination)"-Of-"(Many-"(Pronouns)"

∫many pronouns∫, ∫with the primary exception being the pronoun∫-"(He)"-∫in reference to∫-"The-"(Boy"-"God"-"Con"-"Ta/Al)"-∫as in∫-"The-"(S-(He)"-"(He)"-"(He)-R)"-"(Internal-"(Con)"-Struct)," ∫are eliminated in∫-"Th(e)"-"(Non-"(Con)"-ventional)"-Writing)"-Style)," "(Use)"-Of)"-"(Co-"(L)"-oR)"-"(Cod(e)-ing)"-∫because∫-"The-"(Severely-"(emotionallyIntellectually)"-Unbalanced)"-"(Sh-It/Un-It-"(egO)"-Gods)"-∫of∫-"(Untrue)"-Blue)"-Humanity)"-∫are∫-"(Pros)"-"A"t-"(Defusing)"-"The-"(emotional)"-Crisis)"-Within)"-∫by∫-"(R(e)-lating)"-To-"(each-"(Other)"-In)"-"(A)"-"(Generic)"-"(She)"-"(He)"-"(Her)"-"(Shallow)"-"(Superficial)"-"(Cosmetic)"-"(Outwardly-"(Shiny)"-Manner)." the simple integrated truth is the function∫-"(Pronouns)"-Serve)"-In-"(Interpersonal-"(R(e)-lationships)"-∫is integrated into the word∫-"(PrO-nO-uN)"-∫because∫-"(Being-"(Pro)"-"(nO-"(I)"-A"m-"(Not)"-"(unwanted-unneeded-unloved)"-"(R(e)-quires)"-Assigning)"-"(MoreNot)"-Less)"-Ambiguity)"-∫to∫-"The-"(Discourse)"-"Defining)"-"(Our-"(Interpersonal-"(R(e)-lationship)."

the simple truth is generic pronouns are∫-"(MoreNot)"-Less)"-In-"(Line)"-With)"-"The-"(Con)"-fusion)"-"(Con)"-flict)"-∫associated with∫-"The-"(Gray)"-Zone)"-Of-"(emotional)"-Uncertainty)"-Within)"-∫because∫-"(MoreNot)"-Less)"-"(nO)"-WiL)"-BiL)"-Ambiguity)"-∫on∫-"The-"(Bl-A-cKWh-I-T(e)"-Outside)"-∫helps∫-"(Defuse)"-"The-"(Chances)"-Of)"-"(U)"-"(They"-"Them"-"Those)"-Others)"-"(Noticing)"-"(U)"-"(Have-"(Been-"(Assigned)"-"The-"(Supporting)"-Role)"-∫of∫-"(GivingNot)"-Getting)"-"(enough-"(Affection"-"Attention"-"Approval)"-To-"(Verify)"-"(I)"-"("A"m-"(Worthy)"-Of-"(Being)"-∫lovnewed∫. the simple truth is∫most pronouns are eliminated from the text∫because pronouns are used in∫-"(A)"-"(Con)"-text)"-Of-"(Denial)"-∫which∫-"(Allows)"-"(the-Orange-(emotional)-Flame)-Driven)"-"(I)"-"(Cons)"-∫to∫-"(Con)"-bine)"-everyone)"-Into)"-"(A)"-"(Homogeneous)"-"(She)"-"(He)"-"(Her)"-"(Traveling-"(e)N-Mass)"-Mass)"-To-"(Avoid)"-"The-"(Unpleasant)"-Task)"-Of-"(Dealing)"-With)"-"The-"(Gray)"-Zone)"-"(e)N-igma)"-Of-"(Self)"-Within)."

"(Restricted)"-Use)"-Of-"(Possessive)"-Words)"

"(Restricted)"-Use)"-Of-"(Possessives)"-"(Possessive)"-Pronouns)"

"(Restricted)"-Use)"-⸗applies to all⸗-"(Possessive)"-Words)"-⸗to help the reader understand⸗-"(Having-"(Possessive)"-"(Con)"-trolling)"-"(R(e)-lationships),"-"(Trying)"-To-"(Possess)"-"(MoreNot)"-Less)"-"(Objects)"-"(Things)"-"(egO)"-tistical)"-Materialism)"-⸗for⸗-"(emotional)"-Security)"-Within)"-⸗will not change⸗-"The-"(Severe-"(emotionalIntellectual)"-Unbalanced)"-"(Con)"-dition)"-Within)"-"(One-"(Iota)"-⸗because⸗-"The-"(Severe-"(emotionalIntellectual)"-Unbalanced)"-"(Con)"-dition)"-⸗is on⸗-"The-"(Bl-A-cKWh-I-T(e)"-Inside)"-⸗not⸗-"The-"(Bl-A-cK Wh-I-T(e)"-Outside)." the simple truth is restricted use of⸗-"(Possessives)"-"(Possessive)"-Pronouns)"-⸗is intended to help⸗-"(Humanity)"-⸗understand⸗-"(Possessiveness)," "(Possessions)"-⸗do not exist in⸗the life of the internally passioned trusting⸗tender⸗truthful true blue individual being me⸗because the one true god⸗the me did not integrate⸗-"The-"(Quality)"-Of-"(Being-"(Possessive)," "The-"(D(e)-"(S.I.R.)"-(e)"-To-"(Own)"-"(Possess)"-⸗into ⸗the gene code of humanity⸗.

"(Con)"-tractions)"

"(elimination)"-Of-"(Con)"-tractions)"

all⸗-"(Con)"-tractions)"-⸗are eliminated to help the reader⸗understand⸗, "(Although)"-"The-"(Con)"-tract)"-With)"-"The-"(Boy)"-"God"-"Con"-"Ta/Al)"-"(Allows)"-"The-"(Proud)"-"(I)"-"(Cons)"-To-"(Use-"(Gods)"-That-"(Are-"(external)"-To)"-⸗the trusting⸗tender⸗truthful path of the one true god⸗the me⸗deep within⸗, trying to⸗-"(Abbreviate)"-⸗the necessity⸗to change from within⸗by using⸗-"The-"(Short)"-Cut)"-Of-"(Ta/Al)"-"(external-"(Gods)"-⸗will not⸗-"(eliminate)"-"The-"(emotional)"-Pain/Suffering)"-Within)"-⸗because⸗-"The-"(emotional)"-Pain/Suffering)"-⸗associated with⸗-"(the-black-emotional-hole-within)"-⸗can only be removed by first⸗accepting⸗acknowledging⸗admitting⸗being⸗-"(Severely-"(emotionallyIntellectually)"-Unbalanced)." the simple integrated truth in⸗-"(I)'m"-"The-"(Con)"-traction)"-For-"(I)"-"A"m)"-⸗is⸗-"The-"(Capital)"-Letter)"-"(A)"-⸗is⸗-"(Con)"-spicuously)"-Absent)"-⸗in⸗-"The-"(Con)"-traction)"-⸗because instead of⸗accepting⸗acknowledging⸗admitting⸗being⸗-"(Severely-"(emotionallyIntellectually)"-Unbalanced)," "The-"(I)"-"(Cons)"-"(Proudly)"-"Proclaim)"-"(I)"-"A"m-"(Being-"(M(e)"-By-"(Simply-"(Honoring)"-"The-"(Con)"-tract)"-With)"-"The-"(Boy)"-"God"-"Con"-"Ta/Al)"-To-"(Use)"-"(Any-"(Quick)"-"(external-"(Fix)"-⸗for⸗-"The-"(emotional)"-Dilemma)"-Within)."

"(Con)"-junctions)"

"(eliminating)"-"The-"(Three-"(Major-"(Con)"-junctions)"-"(And)"-"(But)"-"(Or)"

"The-"(Con)"-junctions)," "(And)"-"(But)"-"(Or)"-∫are eliminated in∫-"Th(e)"-"(Non-"(Con)"-ventional)"-Writing)"-Style)," "(Use)"-Of)"-"(Co-"(L)"-oR)"-"(Cod(e)-ing)"-∫because∫-"(Con)"-junctions)"-"(Serve)"-"The-"(Boy)"-"God"-"Con"-"Ta/Al)"-"Function)"-Of-"(Making-"(Self)"-Serving)"-"(Seemingly-"(Logical)"-"(And)"-"(But)"-"(Or)"-Modifications)"-To)"-∫the simple truth of being∫-"(Severely-"(emotionally Intellectually)"-Divided)"-Within)." "The-"(Boy)"-"God"-"Con"-"Ta/Al)"-"(Knows)"-"(It)"-Is-"(Only-"(Logical)"-To-"(Make)"-"The-"(And-"(Con)"-nection)"-Between)"-"(U)"-"(They)"-"Them"-"Those"-Others)"-"(And)"-"(I)"-∫on∫-"The-"(Bl-A-cK Wh-I-T(e)"-Outside)"-∫because∫-"(Making)"-"(A)"-"(Con)"-nection)"-With"-"(U)"-"(By-"(Joining)"-"(A)"-"(Mc-W(e)Mc-uS)"-Flock)"-With-"(Similar-"(Values)"-"(Morals)"-"(Mores)"-∫on∫-"The-"(Bl-A-cK Wh-I-T(e)"-Outside)"-"(Provides)"-"The-"(Pro-Wry-Dr.-"(I)"-"(Proud)"-"(I)"-"(Cons)"-With-"(enough)"-"(emotional)"-Security)"-"(To-"(Con)"-nect)"-"The-"(emotionalIntellectual)"-"(Dis-"(Junction)"-∫on∫-"The-"(Bl-A-cK Wh-I-T(e)"-Inside)".

"The-"(Boy)"-"God"-"Con"-"Ta/Al)"-"(Con)"-Job)"-"(Serves)"-"The-"(Boy)"-"God"-"Con"-"Ta/Al)"-Function)"-Of-"(Allowing)"-∫the simple truth∫-"(Con)"-trarians)"-To-"(Proudly)"-Proclaim)-Being)"-"(A)"-"(O.K.)"-"(just)"-Fine)"-∫because as long as∫-"The-"(Boy)"-"God"-"Con"-"Ta/Al)"-Is-"(Allowed)"-To-"(Use)"-"The-"(Purple)"-Haze)"-Dazed)"-"(But)"-Logic)"-Of-"(But-"(I)"-"A"m)"-"(A)"-"(BiGNot)"-small)"-"(egO)"-tistical)"-Somebody)"-∫on∫-"The-"(Bl-A-cK Wh-I-T(e)"-Outside)," "The-"(feeling-oh-so-small)"-"(nO)"-WiL)"-BiLs)"-∫will∫-"(R(e)-main)"-"(Severely-"(emotionallyIntellectually)"-Unbalanced)"-∫on∫-"The-"(Bl-A-cK Wh-I-T(e)"-Inside)." the simple truth is∫-"The-"(Boy)"-"God"-"Con"-"Ta/Al)"-"(Con)"-Job)"-"(Serves)"-"The-"(Function)"-Of-"(Finding)"-"A"n-"(Or)"-Alternative)"-∫to ∫accepting∫ acknowledging∫admitting∫being∫-"(Severely-"(emotionallyIntellectually)"-Unbalanced)"-∫because∫-"The-"(Boy)"-"God"-"Con"-"Ta/Al)"-"(Sink-Or-Swim)"-"(Mentality)"-Includes-"(Trying)"-To-"(Lessen)"-"The-"(Gray)"-Zone)"-Of-"(emotional)"-Uncertainty)"-∫associated with∫-"(not-feeling-worthy-of-being)"-∫lovne wed∫by∫-"(Substituting)"-"The-"(Con)"-trarian)"-"(Boy)"-"God"-"Con"-"Ta/Al)"-"Logic)"-Of-"(Finding-"(enough)"-"(emotional)"-Security)"-∫in∫-"(This-Or-That)"-"(external)"-Solution)"-To-"(Avoid)"-"The-"(Unpleasant)"-Task)"-Of-"(Facing)"-∫the simple truth of being∫-"(Severely-"(eI)"-Unbalanced)"-Within)."

15

grammatical rule

not following the rule of eliminating – "The-"(e)" – if adding a suffix

"Th(e)"-"(Non-"(Con)"-ventional)"-Writing)"-Style)," "(Use)"-Of)"-"(Co-"(L)"-oR)"-"(Cod(e)-ing)"-does not always follow the grammatical rule of eliminating-"The-"(e)"-if adding a suffix, as in-"(Approve)"-becoming-"(Approval)"-because-"(earning)"-"The-"(Ap-Pr-O-V(e)-aL)"-of-"(U)"-(They"-"Them"-"Those)"-Others)"-Includes-"(Con)"-cealing)"-"The-"(Boy"-"God"-"Con"-"Ta/Al)"-"(Secret-"(egO)"-Garden)"-"(Secret)"-Of-"(Being)"-"The-"(egO)"-tistical)"-"(It)," integrated into-"The-"(e)"-in-"(Ap-Pr-O-V(e)-aL)." the one true god-the me asks-"(Untrue)"-Blue)"-Humanity)"-to try to-understand," while-"(Con)"-cealing)"-"The-"(Boy"-"God"-"Con"-"Ta/Al)"-"(Secret-"(egO)"-Garden)"-"(Secret)"-Of-"(Being)"-"The-"(egO)"-tistical)"-"(It)"-"(may)"-(Help-"(earn)"-"The-"(Ap-Pr-O-V(e)-aL)"-of-"(U)"-(They"-"Them"-"Those)"-Others)," "(Pro-Wry-Dr.-"(I)"-"Presenting)"-"A"n-"(especially-"(Con)"-Passionate)"-"(Con)"-Curious)"-"(Con)"-Courageous)"-"(Perfect-Pearl-"(He)"-Art-Act)"-That-"(earns-"(enough-"(Well-"(Deserved)"-"(Affection"-"Approval"-"Attention)"-"(Without-"(exposing)"-"(Being)"-"The-"(egO)"-tistical)"-"(It)"-is-"(especially-"(Futile)"-because-"The-"(Boy"-"God"-"Con"-"Ta/Al)"-"(egO)"-tistical)"-Fix)"-for-"(the-black-emotional-hole-within)"-is-"The-"(Problem)," not-"The-"(Solution)."

sentence structure

the simple truth is-because sentence structure

the simple truth is-because sentence structure is being used to help-"-(Humanity)"-understand-the reason-"The-"(Boy"-"God"-"Con"-"Ta/Al)"-has-"-(R(e)-placed)"-being true blue curious enough to ask why with the true blue-purity of intent-"(With-"(Con)"-Curiosity)," "The-"(Intellectualized)"-Version)"-of-true blue curiosity-is because of-"The-"(Generational)"-effect)"-Of)"-"(Bl-A-cK-Wh-I-T(e)"-(Parenting)"-With-"(Fear)," "(A)"-"(Lack)"-Of)"-Iamal-"(before-the-age-of-two)"-because-"(Generations)"-Of)"-"(Bl-A-cK-Wh-I-T(e)"-(Parenting)"-With-"(Fear)," "(A)"-"(Lack)"-Of)"-Iamal-has made-"(Con)"-Curiosity)"-"(A)"-"(Critical)"-"(Perfect-Pearl-"(He)"-Art-Act)"-"(Con)"-ponent)."

"(Substitution)"

"(Substituting)"-"(Con)"-⌠for com,

"(Con)"-⌠is substituted for com, a prefix meaning united⌠together, as in compassion becoming⌠-"(Con)"-Passion)"-⌠to help the reader⌠understand⌠, instead of being ⌠emotionally⌠intellectually united⌠balanced within⌠, "The-"(Life)"-⌠of⌠the internally passioned⌠trusting⌠tender⌠truthful⌠true blue humble⌠compassionate⌠curious⌠ courageous⌠zestful individual me at birth⌠becomes⌠-"(A)"-"(Con)"-Passionate)"- "(Con)"-Job)"-"(before-the-age-of-two)"-⌠because⌠-"The-"(Boy"-"God"-"Con"- "Ta/Al)"-"(Con)"-pensates)"-For-"(Being)"-⌠(Parented)"-⌠With-"(Fear)," "(A)"- "(Lack)"-Of"-⌠Jamal -⌠(before-the-age-of-two)"-⌠by⌠-"(Using)"-"The-"(Con)"- Passionate)"-"(J)"-Hook)"-To-"(Intellectually)"-"(earn-"(enough-"(Affection"- "Approval"-"Attention)"-From-"(U)"-To-"(Feel-"(Worthy)"-Of-"(Being)"-⌠lovnewed⌠.

"(Word)"-Separation)"

"(Separating)"-Words)"-"(Starting)"-With-"(Con)"-With)"-"(A)"-"(Dash)"

the dash is used to separate words beginning with⌠-"(Con)," such as connection⌠ confusion⌠conflicted⌠confounded⌠congregation becoming⌠-"(Con)"-nection)," "(Con)"- fusion)," "(Con)"-flicted)," "(Con)"-founded)," "(Con)"-gregation)"-⌠to help the reader ⌠understand⌠-"The-"(Con)"-Job)"-⌠associated with⌠-"The-"(Boy"-"God"-"Con"- "Ta/Al)"-"(egO)"-Bridge)"-Fix)"-⌠because⌠-"The-"(Boy"-"God"-"Con"-"Ta/Al)"- "(Tries)"-To-"(Make)"-"A"n-"(Affection"-"Approval"-"Attention)"-"(Con)"-nection)"- With)"-"(This-(e)R-That)"-"(Mc-W(e)Mc-uS)"-"(Con)"-gregation)"-To-"(Lessen)"- "The-"(Con)"-fusion)"-"(Sense)"-Of-"(Being-"(Con)"-founded)"-"(Con)"-flicted)"- ⌠associated with⌠-"The-"(Gray)"-Zone)"-Of-"(emotional)"-Uncertainty)."

"(Inter-"(R(e)-lationship)"

"The-"(Inter-"(R(e)-lationship)"-Between-"(Words)"

the simple integrated truth in⌠-"The-"(Capital)"-Letter)"-"(A)"-Matrix)"-⌠on page 18 defines⌠-"The-"(Intent)"-⌠of⌠-"The-"(Sh-It/Un-It-"(egO)"-Gods)"-⌠of⌠-"(Untrue)"- Blue)"-Humanity)"-⌠because⌠-"The-"(Capital)"-Letter)"-"(A)⌠defines⌠-"The-"(Severe- "(emotional⌠Intellectual)"-Unbalanced)"-"(Con)"-dition)"-Within)"-⌠the emotionally intellectually balanced child at birth⌠. the center column in⌠-"The-"(Capital)"-Letter)"- "(A)"-Matrix)"-⌠written in⌠-"Th(e)"-"(Non-"(Con)"-ventional)"-Writing)"-Style),"

17

"(Use)"-Of)" -"(Co-"(L)"-oR)" -"(Cod(e)-ing)" -∫is intended to help∫-"(Humanity)"- ∫understand the life of the individual being me at birth∫becomes an∫-"(Affection"- "Approval"-"Attention)"-"(Seeking-"(C-O-N)"-Job)" -∫because although∫the gene code of each∫every individual in the we of all humanity∫does not include being∫-"(egO)"- tistical), "The-"(Generational)"-effect)"-Of)" -"(Bl-A-cK∫Wh-I-T(e)"-"(Parenting)"- "(With-"(Fear)," "(A)" -"(Lack)"-Of)" -∫amal∫-"(before-the-age-of-two)" -"(R(e)-sults)"- In)"-"The-"(Boy"-"God"-"Con"-"Ta/Al)"-"(Trying)"-To-"(Perfect)"-"A"n- "(Affection"-"Approval"-"Attention)"-"(Seeking-"(Con)"-Job)"-To-"(Feel-"(Worthy)"- Of-"(Being)" -∫lovnewed∫.

the right column lays bare the simple truth about∫-"The-"(R(e)-lationship)" -∫between∫- "(I)" -"(U)" -∫is∫-"(Con)"-trolled)"-By-"(Ta)" -∫because∫-"(Ta)"-"(Uses)"-"(U)" -∫to∫- "(AcH-"(I)" -(e)V(e)"-"(At-"(Ta)"-iN)" -"(AcQ-"(U)"-Ir(e)" -∫an∫-"(Uneasy-"(Peace)"- For)" -"(the-"(Orange-(emotional)-Flame)" -of-"(Yellowish-Fear∫Seeing-Red-Anger)- within)." the simple integrated truth in the left column is∫-"The-"(Proud)" -"(I)" - "(Cons)" -∫will not∫-"(Ac-C(e)-pT)," "(AcK-nO-(w)-L(e)-Dg(e)," "(Ad-M-iT)" -∫being∫- "(Severely-"(emotionally∫Intellectually)"-Unbalanced)"-Within)" -∫because∫-"The-"(e)T- Pt/P(e)-T(e)" -"(Sh-It/Un-It-"(egO)"-Gods)" -"(Use)"-"The-"(e)M)"-Ad)"-To-"(Both- "(Con)"-ceal)"-"(Being)" -"The-"(egO)"-tistical)"-"(It)," "(earn-"(enough-"(Affection"- "Approval"-"Attention)"-To-"(Deny)"-"(Being)" -"(A)" -"(worthless-useless-unwanted- unneeded-unloved-nobody)."

the simple integrated truth in∫-"The-"(Capital)"-Letter)"-"(A)"-Matrix)"

"(Ac-C(e)-pT)"   "(Af-F(e)-"C"-tI-oN)"   "(AcH-"I"-(e)V(e)"

"(AcK-nO-(w)-L(e)-Dg(e)"   "(Ap-Pr-"O"-V(e)-aL)"   "(At-"Ta"-iN)"

"(Ad-M-iT)"   "(At-T(e)-"N"-tI-oN)"   "(AcQ-"U"-Ir(e)"

"(Co-L-oR)" - "(Cod(e)-ing)"

the simple integrated truth is the color lavender, a tertiary color comprised of the three colors, red white blue, is being used as the background color for the text because the vibrational essence of the child at play in the field of lavender hue deep within me was created to be a beautiful lavender hue. the simple truth is if the individuals in the we of all humanity were playing in the field of lavender hue within, the skies of the home planet would be a beautiful lavender hue because the collective vibrational essence associated with the red white blue integrated into the field of lavender hue deep within composed of being internally passioned trusting tender truthful true blue humble compassionate curious courageous zestful is a beautiful lavender hue.

the simple integrated truth is a white background is used in association with the child at play in the field of lavender hue deep within the individual being me because the white background color visually supports the simple truth of the we of all humanity being integrated into the one true god the me of the trust tenderness truth. the integral symbol, ∫, is also color coded white to visually support the simple truth of the creator of humanity being an integral part of the universe because the universe the home planet the we of all humanity are integrated into the one true god the me of the trust tenderness truth.

the white color coded attribute of being trusting tender truthful in the gene code of humanity is the path the creator of the we of all humanity uses to try to guide each every individual on the home planet from within because the cells making up the trusting tender truthful path are vibrationally sensitive to the trusting tender truthful whisper of the one true god the me of the trust tenderness truth. although the we of all humanity is integrated into the one true god the me, the emotionally intellectually balanced child at birth must choose with the blessing of free will to allow the one true god the me to guide me from within because the integration of free will into the gene code of humanity means the creator must ask, cannot make any human being do anything.

the word lamal, defined as genuine compassionate tender gentle emotional physical touch, the word lovnew are both color coded lavender with a white background to help the reader understand the field of lavender hue deep within must be nurtured with lamal because although the nature of each every individual on the home planet is defined by the field of lavender hue deep within, the child not nurtured with lamal will not feel lovnewed. the simple integrated truth is instead of being the internally passioned trusting tender truthful true blue humble compassionate curious courageous zestful individual me, "The-"(Red)"-(White)"-"(Blue)"- found on the home planet the planet intended to be the planet of lavender hue by the one true god the me is being

19

-"(externally)"-Passioned)" - "(egO)"-tistical)" - "(Cold)" - "(egO)"-"(e)M-otionless)" - ∫because∫the field of lavender hue deep within∫was not∫nurtured with lamal∫.

the simple integrated truth is the term∫true blue∫-"(Inert/Noble)"-∫is color coded∫-"(Baby)"-Blue)"-∫because the baby blue color of the sky reflects the vibrational essence associated with∫-"The-"(Internal-"(Con)"-struct)"-Of-"(Being-"(egO)"-tistical)"-"(Cold)"-"(egO)"-"(e)M-otionless)"-Within)." the simple truth is the color red associated with being∫-"(externally)"-Passioned)"-∫is not represented in the baby blue color of the sky because vibrational essence is determined by that which is within, not∫-"(external)"-To)"-∫as is∫-"(external)"-Passion)."

similar to the text elements in∫-"Th(e)"-"(Non-"(Con)"-ventional)"-Writing)"-Style)," "Th(e)"-"(Use)"-Of)"-"(Co-"(L)"-oR)"-"(Cod(e)-ing)"-∫is intended to help the reader ∫understand∫-"The-"(Generational)"-effect)"-Of)"-"(Bl-A-cK∫Wh-I-T(e)"-"(Parenting)"-"(With-"(Fear)," "(A)"-"(Lack)"-Of)"-∫lamal∫-"(before-the-age-of-two)"-∫because the color coding visually supports the intended message. the simple truth is∫the emotionally∫intellectually balanced child at birth∫becomes∫-"(Severely-"(emotionally Intellectually)"-Unbalanced)"-Within)"-∫because∫-"The-"(Boy"-"God"-"Con"-"Ta/Al)," the term used to define∫-"(Intellect)," "(Installs)"-"The-"(egO)"-Bridge)"-To-"(Cope)"-With)"-"(the-black-emotional-hole-problem)." while∫-"(the-black-emotional-hole)"-∫is color coded black, "The-"(Intellect)"-∫represents the white in∫-"The-"(Bl-A-cK∫Wh-I-T(e)"-"(egO)"-Based)"-Internal-"(Con)"-struct)"-∫because∫-"The-"(Boy"-"God"-"Con"-"Ta/Al)"-"(Tries)"-To-"(Solve)"-"(the-black-emotional-hole-problem-of-feeling-worthless-useless-unwanted-unneeded-unloved)"-∫with∫-"The-"(egO)"-Bridge)"-Fix)"-Of-"(Intellectually)"-"(earning-"(Affection"-"Approval"-"Attention)."

the numerous terms used to define∫-"(Intellect)"-∫throughout the text are all color coded white with a black background because the color coding reinforces the simple truth associated with∫-"The-"(Bl-A-cK∫Wh-I-T(e)"-"(egO)"-Based)"-"(Internal-"(Con)"-struct)." the terms defining∫-"(Intellect)"-∫include∫-"The-"(Boy"-"God"-"Con"-"Ta/Al)," "(egO)," "The-"(Malefactor)," "The-"(Reigning-"(Beau)," "The-"(Temple)"-∫between∫the temples∫, "(Con)"-∫as in∫-"(Con)"-Passionate)"-"(Con)"-Curious)"-"(Con)"-Courageous)," "(He)"-∫as in∫-"The-"(Perfect-Pearl-With-Tenish-Angel-Wings-"(He)"-Art-Act)," as well as∫-"The-"(Lord/Master)"-Of-"(the-Orange-(emotional)-Flame)."

the opposite black∫white background color is used on words, such as∫-"(Bl-A-cK∫Wh-I-T(e)"-∫because using a∫-"(White-Background)"-∫in association with a∫-"(Bl-A-cK)"-∫color coded word, a∫-"(Black-Background)"-with a∫-"(Wh-I-T(e)"-∫color coded word is a simple method used to visually support the simple truth integrated into∫-"(Bl-A-cKWh-I-T(e)" -∫by the creator of∫humanity∫. the simple truth integrated into the word∫-"(B-Lack)"-is∫-"(the-black-emotional-hole)"-∫is caused by- (A) -"(Lack)"-Of"-∫lamal∫, the∫-"(La)"-∫in∫-"(B-La-cK)." the simple truth integrated into the word"-"(W-HiT-(e)"-∫is∫-"(Instead-Of-"(Taking-"(A)"-"(HiT)"-For-"(Being)"-"The-"(egO)"-tistical)"-"(It), "The-"(Proud)"-∫-(I)"-∫(Cons)"-∫-Use)"-∫This-(e)R-That)"-"(W(e)," known as∫-"The-"(Mc-W(e)Mc-uS)"-Flock)," as∫-"(A)"-"(Narcissistic)"-"(R(e)"-flective)"-Pool).

similar to∫-"(the-black-emotional-hole)"-∫being color coded black to visually support the color named in the term, "Th(e)"-"(Co-L-oR)"-∫(Cod(e)-ing)"-∫used for several terms is based upon the color named. the terms include∫-"The-"(Gray)"-Zone)"-Of-"(emotional)"-Uncertainty)," "(the-(Orange-(emotional)-Flame)"-∫comprised of∫-"(the-(Yellowish-Fear)-of-not-feeling-worthy-of-being)"- ∫lovnewed∫, "(the-(Seeing-Red-Anger)-of-not-being-allowed)"- ∫to be me∫, "The-"(Tickled-"(Pink)"-Buds)"-Of-"(egO)"-tistical)"-"White)"-∫(externally)"-Passioned)"-Red)"-Roses)," "The-"(La)"-Venders)"-Of-"(Untrue)"-Blue)"-Humanity)," as well as∫-"(Purple)"-Haze)"-Dazed)." the terms with either a white∫ black background support the simple truth associated with∫-"The-"(Bl-A-cKWh-I-T(e)"-"(egO)"-Based)"-"(Internal-"(Con)"-struct)".

the word∫-"(Parenting)"-∫as in∫-"The-"(Generational)"-effect)"-Of"- "(Bl-A-cKWh-I-T(e)"-"(Parenting)"-∫(With-"(Fear)," "(A)"-"(Lack)"-Of)"-∫lamal∫-"(before-the-age-of-two)"-∫is color coded gray with gray color coded parentheses because unless∫-"(Severely-"(emotionallyIntellectually)"-Unbalanced)"-"(Parents)"-∫make∫the most difficult journey∫the inward journey∫, "The-"(Parents)"-∫will∫-"(Live)"-Life)"-In)"-"The-"(Gray)"-Zone)"-Of-"(emotional)"-Uncertainty)." the simple integrated truth is a white color coded, (e), set in gray color coded parentheses is used at the center of∫-"(PaR-(e)-NtS)"-∫because in addition to each∫-"(Pa-R(e)-nT)"-∫"(Using)"-"The-"(Affection"-"Approval"-"Attention)"-"(earned-"(From)"-"The-"(R(e)-lationship)"-∫to∫-"(feel-"(LessNot)"-More)"-unwanted-unneeded-unloved)," "The-"(Pair)"-∫of∫-"(PaR-(e)-NtS)"-"(Use)"-"(each-"(Other)"-"A"s-"(A)"-"(Narcissistic)"-"(R(e)-flective)"-Pool)"-∫of∫-"My-"(GoodnessNot)"-Badness)"-"(RightnessNot)"-Wrongness)"-"(StrengthNot)"-Weakness).

the use of∫-"(Co-L-oR)"-∫(Cod(e)-ing)"-∫also lays bare∫-"The-"(Same-"(Boy"-"God"-"Con"-"Ta/Al)"-"(egO)"-Bridge)"-Fix)"-Of-"(Trying)"-To-"(Find)"-"A"n-"(external)"-Solution)"-For)"-"The-"(Internal)"-Problem)"-On)"-"(A)"-"(Societal)"-Scale)"-∫because∫-"(Severely-"(emotionallyIntellectually)"-Unbalanced)"-Individuals)"-"(Use)"-"(This-(e)R-That)"-"(Mc-W(e)Mc-uS)"-Flock)"-"A"s)"-"(A)"-"(Narcissistic)"-"(R(e)-flective)"-Pool)"-∫of∫-"My-"(GoodnessNot)"-Badness)"-"(RightnessNot)"-Wrongness)"-"(StrengthNot)"-"(Weakness)." "The-"(feeling-oh-so-smallMust-Be-Oh-sO-"(egO)"-tistically)"-"BiG)"-"(Proud)"-(I)"-"(Cons)"-∫try to∫-"(Feel)"-"(MoreNot)"-Less)"-"(Bl-A-cKWh-I-T(e)"-"(NormalNot)"-Abnormal)," "(MoreNot)"-Less)"-∫like∫

21

-"(WinnersNot)"-Losers)"-⌡in⌡-"The-"(Affection"-"Approval"-"Attention)"-"(Game)"-Of-"(Life)"-By-"(Fitting)"-Into)"-"(This-(e)R-That)"-"(Mc-W(e)Mc-uS)"-Flock)"-⌡because⌡-"The-"(Bl-A-cKWh-I-T(e)"-Saint)"-Ill)"-"(Proud)"-"(I)"-(Cons)"-⌡of⌡-"(Untrue)"-Blue)"-Humanity)"-"(Transform)"-"(the-black-emotional-hole-negative)"-⌡into⌡-"(A)"-"(Bl-A-cKWh-I-T(e)"-(PositiveNot)"-Negative)"-⌡by using⌡-"(This-(e)R-That)"-"(Mc-W(e)Mc-uS)"-Flock)"-⌡for⌡-"(emotional)"-Security)."

in addition to using⌡-"(This-(e)R-That)"-"(Mc-W(e)Mc-uS)"-Flock)"-⌡for⌡-"(emotional)"-Security," which is⌡-"The-"(Boy"-"God"-"Con"-"Ta/Al)"-"(external-"(God)"-Of-"(U)"-Ism)," "The-"(feeling-oh-so-smallMust-Be-Oh-sO-"(egO)"-tistically)"-"BiG"-"(Proud)"-"(I)"-(Cons)"-⌡use several other⌡-"(Gods)"-⌡for⌡-"(emotional)"-Security"-⌡that are external to⌡the lavender field deep within, including⌡-"(external)"-Passion)," "(Matterism)," "(Intellectualism)," "(Tradition)," "(egO)"-tistical)"-Materialism)," "(Organized-"(R(e)-ligion)." the green color coded background used with⌡-"(the-"(Orange-(emotional)-Flame)," the orange color coded background used with⌡-"The-"(Green)," a form of⌡-"The-"(external-"(God)"-Of-"(egO)"-tistical)"-Materialism)"-⌡reinforces the intended message because the background color helps the reader⌡understand⌡-"The-"(Green)," "(Money)"-⌡is often used in⌡-"(A)"-"(Futile)"-Attempt)"-To-"(Quench)"-⌡the-"(Orange-(emotional)-Flame)-within)."

the simple truth is the line where the white color coded background, the black color coded background meet is⌡-"The-"(Sheer)"-Line)"-⌡allowing⌡-"The-"(Me-Too-Meek-Sheep)"-⌡of⌡-"(Untrue)"-Blue)"-Humanity)"-⌡to be⌡-'[SHEARED]'-⌡by⌡-'THE-'[JO-JOCK-'[EGO]'-GODS]'-⌡for⌡-'[MORENOT]'-LESS]'-'[EGO)]'-TISTICAL)]'-⌡because in order to⌡-"(Feel-"(Worthy)"-Of-"(Being)"-⌡lovnewed, "The-"(Me-Too-Meek-Sheep)"-⌡cannot be⌡-"(Bl-A-cKWh-I-T(e)"-"(WrongNot)"-Right)," must always be⌡-"(Bl-A-cKWh-I-T(e)"-"(RightNot)"-Wrong)." "The-"(Sheer)"-Line)"-⌡also allows⌡-"The-"(Sh-It/Un-It-"(egO)"-Gods)," 'THE-'[JO-JOCK-'[EGO)]'-GODS)]'-⌡to be⌡-'{SLAUGHTERED}'-BY-'THE-'{SEVERELY-'{EMOTIONALLYINTELLECTUALLY}'-UNBALANCED}'-'{MIND}'-'{CON}'-TROLLING}'-PIED-PIPERS}'-⌡of⌡-"(Untrue)"-Blue)"-Humanity)"-⌡because⌡-'THE-'{DR.-JEKYLLMR.-HYDE}'-PIED-PIPERS}'-'{PREY}'-UPON}'-"The-"(egO)"-Bridge)"-Fix"-⌡for⌡-"(the-black-emotional-hole-problem-of-"(Yellowish-FearSeeing-Red-Anger)."

the use of⌡-"(Co-L-oR)"-"(Cod(e)-ing)"-⌡is intended to help the reader⌡understand the we of all humanity⌡has been⌡-'H-A-D'-⌡by⌡-"The-"(Generational)"-effect)"-Of)"-"(Bl-A-cKWh-I-T(e)"-"(Parenting)"-"(With-"(Fear)," "(A)"-"(Lack)"-Of)"-⌡lamal⌡-"(before-the-age-of-two)"-⌡because each color coded letter in⌡-'H-A-D'-⌡represents a different⌡-"(Boy"-"God"-"Con"-"Ta/Al)"-"(egO)"-Bridge)"-Fix)"-⌡for⌡-"(the-black-emotional-hole-problem-of-"(Yellowish-FearSeeing-Red-Anger)." 'H-A-D'-⌡is also the title of a book written by the author to help - "(Humanity)" - understand -"The-"(Generational)"-effect)"-Of) -" (Bl-A-cKWh-I-T(e)" -(Parenting) - (With-"(Fear), " (A) -" (Lack)"-Of)" -Jamal -"(before-the-age-of-two)" -Jhas resulted in the we of all humanity being -'H-A-D' -Jin -"(Numerous)"-Ways) -Jbecause -"(Humanity); has been -'H-A-D' -Jby-"The-"(Social"-"Political"-"(e-"(Con)"-omic)"-"Theories)"-Of-"(Noted-"(Philosphers)," 'H-A-D' -Jby -"The-"(Pro-Wry-Dr.-"(I)"-"(Intellectual)"-"Theories)"-"(Pertaining)"-To)" -Jthe simple physical truths of the universe, 'H-A-D' -Jby -"The-"(Medieval)"-"(Medical-"(Con)"-munity), 'H-A-D' -Jby-"The-"(Ji) -'H-A-D)'-"(Cause)" -Jof-"The-"(Holy)"-War)"-"(Monsters)," 'H-A-D' -Jby-"The-"(Boy)"-"God"-"Con"-"Ta/Al)"-"(external-"(God)"-Of-"(Organized-"(R(e)-ligion).

the brown color coded -"(Capital)"-Letter) " -"(A)" -Jset in gray color coded parentheses, a set of -"(White)" -Jcolor coded double quotation marks in -"H-"(A)"-D' -Jrepresents -"The-"(egO)"-tistical"-"(Con)"-dition)"-Of)" -"The "(Sh-It/Un-It-"(egO)" -Gods)" -Jwith -"The-"(Perfect-Pearl-With-Tenish-Angel-Wings-"(He)"-Art-Act)". although -"The "(Sh-It/Un-It-"(egO)" -Gods)" -Jdo not -"(Con)"-pound) -"The-"(Problem) -Jby making a choice with the blessing of free will, "The- (Bl-A-cKWh-I-T(e)"-Saint"-Ill)"-"(Proud)"-"(A"n-"(I)'m-"(Als)" -Jof - (Untrue)"-Blue)"-Humanity" -"(Avoid)"-Jchoosing with the blessing of free will to accept acknowledge admit being -"(Severely-"(emotionallyIntellectually)"-Unbalanced)"-By-"(Running)"-With)" - (This-(e)R-That)" -"(Herd"-"Flock"-"School)" -Jfor -"(emotional)"-Security).

the -'(BOLD)'-BLACK)' -Jcolor coded -'(CAPITAL)'-LETTER)' -'(H)' -Jin -'(H-"(A)"-D -Jrepresents -'THE-'[(S.I.S.-'[(EGO)]'-GODS)]' -Jwith -'THE-'[(BOLD'-'BRASH'-'BRAZEN)]'-'[(JUST-JO-'[(HE)]'-ART-ACT)]' -Jbecause in addition to -"The-"(Generational)"-effect)"-Of) -"(Bl-A-cKWh-I-T(e)" -"(Parenting)"-(With-"(Fear), " (A) -" (Lack)"-Of) -Jamal - (before-the-age-of-two)," "The-"(Severely-"(emotionallyIntellectually)"-Unbalanced) - (Sh-It/Un-It-"(egO)" -Gods)"-Jchoose with the blessing of free will to be -'[(CARBON)]'-BLACK)]' defined as becoming -'[(INTENTIONALLY)]'-'[(UNTRUSTING'-'[(NOT-'[(TENDER)]'-'UNTRUTHFUL)]'-Jwith-'[(A)'-'[(SIMPLE-'[(MENTAL)]'-'PROCLAMATION)]'-OF-'[(EGO)]'-TISTICAL)]'-SUPREMACY)]' while the gray color coded parentheses represent -"The-"(Generational)"-effect)"-Of) -"(Bl-A-cKWh-I-T(e)" -"(Parenting)" -(With-"(Fear)," (A) -" (Lack)"-Of)" -Jamal - (before-the-age-of-two)," the -'[(BOLD)'-WHITE)'-Jcolor coded -'[(BRACKETS)]' [ ], the -'[(BOLD)'-BLACK)'-'(SINGLE)'-QUOTATION)'-MARKS)' ' ', represent the choice made with the blessing of free will.

the -'{(BOLD}-WHITE}'-Jcolor coded -'{(CAPITAL}}-LETTER)}'-'{(D)}'-Jin -'{(H-"(A)"-D)}'-Jrepresents -'THE-'{(CLOCKWORK)}}'-ORANGE)}' -{(MIND)}'-'{(CON)}'-TROLLING)}'-PIED-PIPERS)}'-WITH-'THE-'{(QUINTESSENTIAL)}'-'{(PERFECT-PEARL-{(HE)}'-ART-ACT)}'-Jbecause in addition to ∫-"The-"(Generational)"-effect)"-Of)"-(Bl-A-cKWh-I-T(e)"-"(Parenting)"-∫With-"(Fear)," "(A)"-(Lack)"-Of)"-∫lamal-∫(before-the-age-of-two), "The-"(Severely-"(emotionallyIntellectually)"-Unbalanced)"-"(Sh-It/Un-It-"(egO)"-Gods)"-∫choose with the blessing of free will to become∫-"THE-"{(DEMENTED'-'DELUSIONAL'-'DERANGED)}'-{(DR.-JEKYLLMR.-HYDE)}'-{(EGO)}'-GODS)}'-WITH-'THE-'{(MESSIAH-{(CON)}'-PLEX)}.' while the gray color coded parentheses represent∫-"The-∫(Generational)"-effect)"-Of)"-(Bl-A-cKWh-I-T(e)"-"(Parenting)"-∫With-"(Fear)," "(A)"-(Lack)"-Of)"-∫lamal-∫(before-the-age-of-two)," the∫-'{(BOLD)}'-WHITE)}'-∫color coded∫-'{(BRACES)},' {( )}, the∫-'{(BOLD)}'-WHITE)}'-'{(SINGLE)}'-QUOTATION)}'-MARKS)},' ' ', represent ∫the choice made with the blessing of free will∫.

the∫-"(Blue)"-∫coding used on words, such as the word∫-"(Cold)"-∫associated with∫-"The-"(Severely-"(emotionallyIntellectually)"-Unbalanced)"-"(Sh-It/Un-It-"(egO)"-Gods)," is intended to help the reader∫understand∫-"The-"(Cold)"-"(egO)"-"(e)M-otionless)"-"(egO)"-"(e)M-ptiness)"-∫of∫-"The-"(Sh-It/Un-It-"(egO)"-Gods)"-∫because∫genuine emotion∫is∫-"(Intellectually)"-"(Trapped-"(Behind)"-"The-"(Same-"(Closed-"(emotional)"-Door)"-∫as∫-"(the-(Yellowish-FearSeeing-Red-Anger)." the one true god the me of the trust∫tenderness∫truth asks∫-"The-"(externally)"-Passioned)"-"(egO)"-tistical)" - "(Cold)" - "(egO)"-"(e)M-otionless)" - "(Sh-It/Un-It-"(egO)"-Gods)"-∫of∫-"(Humanity)"-∫to try to∫understand∫not opening∫-"The-"(Closed-"(emotional)"-Door)"-∫means∫-"The-"(Bl-A-cKWh-I-T(e)"-Saint)"-Ill)"-"(Proud)"-"(I)"-"(Cons)"-∫will not∫find genuine happiness∫joy∫fulfillment within∫because ∫genuine happiness∫joy∫fulfillment will∫-"(R(e)-main)"-"(Trapped-"(Behind)"-"The-"(Closed-"(emotional)"-Door)."

∫the table on page 25 summarizes∫the integrated meaning∫of the colors used in∫-"Th(e)"-"(Non-"(Con)"-ventional)"-Writing)"-Style)," "(Use)"-Of)"-"(Co-"(L)"-oR)"-"(Cod(e)-ing)"-∫which visually support∫the simple integrated truth found in the words because∫-"Th(e)"-"(Use)"-Of)"-"(Co-"(L)"-oR)"-"(Cod(e)-ing)"-∫does not give the reader∫-"The-"(Option)"-Of-"(Intellectually)"-"Assigning)"-"(A)"-"(Meaning)"-To)"-∫the words that is not in agreement with the simple integrated truth. the orange yellow red colors associated with∫-"(the-Orange-(emotional)-Flame)"-∫comprised of∫-"(the-(Yellowish-Fear)-of-not-feeling-worthy-of-being)"-∫lovnewed∫, "(the-(Seeing-Red-Anger)-of-not-being-allowed)"-∫to be the individual me∫for example help the reader∫understand∫the simple integrated truth found in the words because∫-"Th(e)"-"(Co-"(L)"-oR)"-"(Cod(e)-ing)"-∫used supports the simple truth integrated into∫human language∫by the creator of∫humanity∫.

color	the simple integrated truth of the one true god∫the me
black	"(the-black-emotional-hole)"-associated with∫-(Bl-A-cKWh-I-T(e)"-"(Parenting)"-"With-"(Fear)," "(A)"-"(Lack)"-Of)"-∫amal
White	"The-"(egO)"-tistical)"-"(Con)"-ponent)"-∫of∫-(Bl-A-cKWh-I-T(e)"-"(Parenting)"-"With-"(Fear)," "(A)"-"(Lack)"-Of)"-∫amal
Orange	"(the-(Orange-(emotional)-Flame)-deep-within)"
Yellow	"(the-(Yellowish-Fear)"-associated with∫-"(the-(Orange-(emotional)-Flame)"
Red	"(the-(Seeing-Red-Anger)"-associated with∫-"(the-(Orange-(emotional)-Flame)"
Gray	"The-"(Gray)"-Zone)"-Of-"(emotional)"-Uncertainty)"
Pink	"The-"(Tickled-"(Pink)"-Bud)"-∫of∫-"(egO)"-tistical)"-White)"-"(externally)"-Passioned)"-Red)"-Roses)"
Baby Blue	"The-true blue-"(Inert/Noble)"-"(I)"-"(Con)"
Brown	"The-"(Sh-It/Un-It-"(egO)"-Gods)"-∫of∫-"(Untrue)"-Blue)"-Humanity)"
Purple	"The-"(Purple)"-Haze)"-Daze)"-∫of being∫-"(Cold)"-"(egO)"-"(e)M-otionless)"-"(externally)"-Passioned)"
Blue	"The-"(Cold)"-"(egO)"-"(e)M-otionless)"-"(egO)"-"(e)M-ptiness)"-∫of∫-"The-"(Sh-It/Un-It-"(egO)"-Gods)"
Red	"The-"(Boy)"-"God)"-"Con)"-"Ta/Al)"-"(external)"-God)"-∫of∫-"(external)"-Passion)"
Lavender	"The-"(La)"-Vending)"-"Human)"
Green	"The-"(Boy)"-"God)"-"Con)"-"Ta/Al)"-"(external)"-God)"-Of-"(egO)"-tistical)"-Materialism)"-∫in∫-"The-"(Form-"(A)"-Form)"-∫of∫-"The-"(Green)"
BOLD BLACK	'THE-'[(BOLD'-'BRASH'-'BRAZEN)]'-'[(CARBON)]'-BLACK)]'-'[(JO-JOCK-'[(EGO)]'-GODS)]'
BOLD WHITE	'THE-'{(LAN'-'NET'-'WEB}'-'{(MIND)}'-'{(CON)}'-TROLLING)}'-PIED-PIPERS)}'
white	the trusting∫tender∫truthful essence of the one true god∫the me
lavender	the child at play in the field of lavender hue deep within me
red	the internal passion component∫in∫the lavender field deep within me
white	the trusting∫tender∫truthful path in∫the lavender field deep within me
deep blue	the true blue component∫in∫the lavender field deep within of being the true blue humble∫compassionate∫curious∫courageous∫zestful individual me

25